This book belongs to

_____

Goodnight Stories

from the Life of the
Prophet
Muhammad ﷺ

Editor: Maria Skakuj Puri
Illustrated by Gurmeet
First published 2006
Reprinted 2018
© Goodword Books 2018

Goodword Books
A-21, Sector 4, Noida-201301, India
Tel. +9111-46010170, +9111-49534795
Mob. +91-8588822672
email: info@goodwordbooks.com
www.goodwordbooks.com

Chennai
Mob. +91-9790853944, 9600105558

Printed in India

Goodnight Stories
from the Life of the
Prophet
Muhammad ﷺ

SANIYASNAIN KHAN

Goodword

CONTENTS

5

Nursed in the Desert

The Prophet Muhammad ﷺ was not yet born when his father, Abdullah, died. Amina, the Prophet Muhammad's mother, was left alone. When the little boy was born she was very happy. She thought of her baby as being very special. There was a custom among the Arabs of that time for little children to be brought up in the desert. They thought that was best for them. So they sent them to live with the desert tribal women, who looked after these foster children as their own.

Halima Sadia and her family lived in the desert. They were very poor. Their donkey was very old and their she-camel gave no milk. Halima had a little son, but he was always hungry. She had no milk to give him.

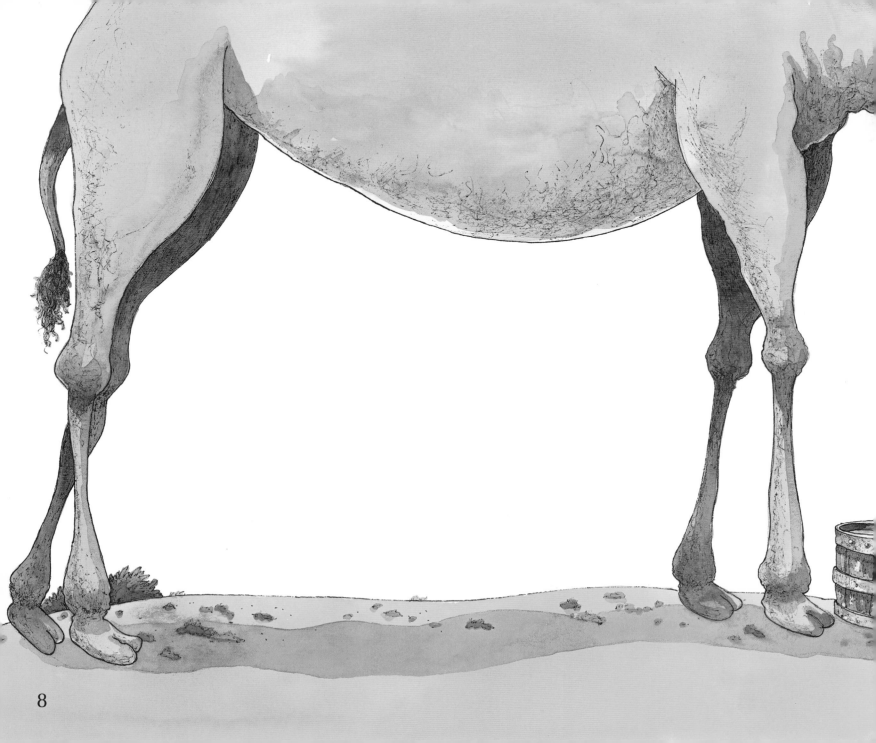

8

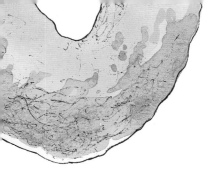

Halima came to Makkah with some other desert women. The townspeople gave their children to these women to take to the desert. The Prophet Muhammad's grandfather, 'Abdu'l Muttalib, was also looking for a nurse for his grandson. But the desert women did not want to take little Muhammad ﷺ. They thought: "He is an orphan. His grandfather and his mother have nothing." It was already evening and Halima had not found any child to take with her. So she said to her husband: "Let me take that orphan boy with me. Nobody wants to take him." Her husband said: "Do it. Maybe Allah will bless us because of him." Halima then took charge of little Muhammad ﷺ and they left Makkah.

They only stopped when they reached the desert. Halima's husband went to milk the she-camel. He cried in surprise: "The she-camel has lots of milk!" All of them drank the milk and then happily went to sleep. In the morning Halima's husband said: "Halima, you have taken a blessed boy." Halima's friends were surprised at how Halima's camel was now giving lots of milk. And Halima's old donkey started being able to walk very fast.

Halima's tribe lived in a barren stretch of desert where nothing grew. All of them often went hungry.

But when little Muhammad ﷺ came to live with them, everything changed. Now Halima's sheep and her camel always had lots of milk. People began to say: "Let's graze our sheep and our camels where Halima takes her flocks. Her animals are well fed. And they always give lots of milk."

Muhammad ﷺ grew up and returned to his mother. But his mother died soon afterwards. He then went to live with his grandfather, 'Abdu'l Muttalib. When he died, the Prophet's uncle, Abu Talib, became his guardian.

Rebuilding Kabah

It was in the thirty fifth year of the Prophet's life that the Quraysh decided to rebuild the Kabah. The Quraysh, who lived in Makkah, were its guardians. They asked a skilled carpenter of Makkah to make a new roof. But for this, they needed timber. It so happened that a ship belonging to a Greek merchant had run aground. As it was a total wreck, the Quraysh took some of its timber. And so the roof was made as they had planned.

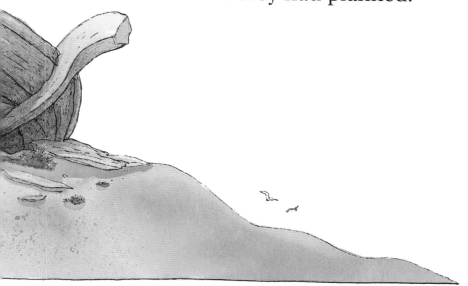

To put on the roof, they had first to demolish the old walls. To begin with, they were afraid to do this lest Allah be angry with them. But finally, they went ahead with their plans, and started re-building the walls. But before they could be completed, the Black Stone had to be put back in its place. This was the most important and most honourable task. Each one of them wanted the honour of fixing the Black Stone in the wall. So they started to fight among themselves. But the more they fought, the less they could agree as to who should put back the Black Stone. Finally, the eldest among them said: "Let the first man who enters the gate next morning judge between us."

At that moment the Prophet Muhammad ﷺ entered the gate. When they saw him, they were very happy. They said: "Here is Muhammad ﷺ. He is the trustworthy one."

Muhammad ﷺ said to the men: "Give me a cloak." Then he put the Black Stone on the cloak. Then he said: "Let each tribe hold one end of the cloak. Now all of you lift it together." All of them lifted the cloak with the Black Stone.

The Prophet Muhammad ﷺ then picked up the Black Stone with his own hands. And he placed the Black Stone on the wall. Then the men went on building the walls higher and higher. Finally they put on the roof. The Kabah was ready.

18

In the Cave of Hira

The Prophet Muhammad ﷺ lived in Makkah with his wife Khadijah. He was a good and honest man. People called him "Al-Amin" which means, the Trustworthy One.

He was a very honest merchant. Like other merchants of Makkah, he traveled far and wide. He went even as far as Syria with the caravans.

On his travels he crossed scorching deserts. He climbed barren hills. He saw beautiful green fields and orchards. He looked at the clear blue sky in the daytime. And he gazed at the stars and the moon at night. And he thought: "Allah has made a beautiful world."

Sometimes Muhammad ﷺ left his friends and family. He traveled to empty spots around Makkah. He sat alone and looked around. He looked at the hills and the valleys. He looked at the trees and the flowers. And he asked himself: "How can we know the Lord of the World? What should we do to make Him pleased with us? How was the world made? Where do people come from? And where do they go after death?"

There was a hill side near Makkah in which there was a cave called the Cave of Hira. Every year in the month of Ramadan, Prophet Muhammad ﷺ went to this cave.

He spent the whole month thinking and praying. Allah made him love
solitude, so that he liked nothing better than to be alone.

In the year 610 the Prophet Muhammad ﷺ was forty years old.
As usual, that year also he went to the cave of Hira to spend Ramadan.

At night, while the Prophet Muhammad ﷺ was sitting, the Angel Jibril
(Gabriel) came to him.

He said: "Recite!" Prophet Muhammad ﷺ asked: "What should I recite?" Jibril again said: "Recite!" The Prophet ﷺ again refused. He did not know what he should recite.

Jibril said: "Recite in the name of your Lord Who created – created man from clots of blood. Recite! Your Lord is the Most Bountiful One, Who by the pen taught man what he did not know."

The Prophet Muhammad ﷺ then recited the words. Then Jibril left him. The Prophet Muhammad ﷺ was again alone. He felt the words he had just recited were written down in his heart.

The Prophet Muhammad ﷺ began shaking with fear. He started to walk down the mountain. Then he heard a voice again: "Muhammad! You are the messenger of Allah. And I am Jibril."

The Prophet Muhammad ﷺ looked up. It was the same man he had seen in the cave. It was not really a man, but the Angel Jibril.

This was the first revelation made to the Prophet Muhammad ﷺ. Jibril taught him the first verses of the Quran. The words entered the Prophet Muhammad's heart. And he became the Messenger of Allah.

The Story of Faithful Khadijah

The Prophet Muhammad ﷺ belonged to the tribe of the Quraysh. He was an orphan. His father died before he was born. His mother died when he was a young child. He began to live with his grandfather, Abdu'l Muttalib. And after

the death of his grandfather, his uncle, Abu Talib became his guardian. But Allah looked after him.

Muhammad ﷺ was a very hardworking and honest man. The people of Makkah called him "Al-Amin", which means the Trustworthy One. He worked for the Quraysh traders, traveling with their caravans across the desert.

Now Khadijah at that time ranked highest among the Quraysh. She was very dignified and also very rich. She was a widow and looked after her business herself. She heard that Muhammad ﷺ was a very honest person. She said to him: "Take my goods to Syria and trade them there. Buy other goods with the money you get and bring them to Makkah."

Muhammad ﷺ took the goods to Syria, sold them there, and with the money he got, he bought other goods for Khadijah.

When Khadijah sold these goods in Makkah she made lots of profit. She liked Muhammad's honesty. And she married him.

The Prophet Muhammad ﷺ and Khadijah had two sons, Qasim and Abdullah. But both of them died when they were very small. They also had four daughters: Zaynab, Ruqayyah, Umm Kulthum and Fatimah. All the daughters lived to see their father become the Messenger of Allah.

One day the Prophet Muhammad ﷺ went to the Cave of Hira. Suddenly Jibril appeared before him. He taught the Prophet verses from the Quran. He said: "Muhammad! You are the Messenger of Allah."

The Prophet Muhammad ﷺ got frightened. He could not believe that Allah had sent an angel to him. He could not believe that Allah would choose him as His messenger.

He went home and told Khadijah: "Something strange has happened to me. An angel of Allah called Jibril came and spoke to me. I cannot believe that Allah sent Jibril to speak to me. I cannot believe Allah wants me to be His Messenger."

31

But Khadijah had no doubts. She said: "You are honest. And you are trustworthy. Allah knows that you are honest and trustworthy. Surely Allah has made you a prophet to your people. I believe in Allah and I believe in the revelation He gave you."

Khadijah was the very first person to hear what had happened in the cave of Hira. She was the very first person to accept Islam. She was the greatest support to the Prophet as long as she lived. Allah honoured her with many great virtues. And she was Allah's faithful servant.

The First Converts

When the Prophet Muhammad ﷺ returned from the cave of Hira, he told his wife, Khadijah: "An angel came to me. He taught me verses from the Qur'an. And he also told me that I am a messenger of Allah."

Khadijah said to the Prophet: "You are good and honest. Allah has made you His prophet. There is no doubt about it." And she became the first person to accept Islam.

There was a little boy living with Muhammad ﷺ and Khadijah. He was about ten years old and his name was Ali. His father, Abu Talib, was the Prophet's uncle.

When Muhammad ﷺ received the revelation from Allah, he told Khadijah about it. Immediately she became a Muslim. When Ali came to know what had happened in the cave of Hira, he also accepted Islam. One day Abu Talib asked Muhammad ﷺ: "Nephew, what is this religion you practice?"

Muhammad ﷺ said: "Uncle, this is the religion of Allah. This is the religion of His messengers. And this is the religion of our father Abraham." Then Abu Talib asked his son Ali: "Son, what is this religion of yours?"

Ali said: "I believe in Allah, and the Messenger of Allah, and I say: what the messenger says is true. I pray to Allah with him and follow him." Abu Talib did not accept Islam. But he supported Muhammad ﷺ against his enemies as long as he lived.

After Khadijah and Ali more people accepted Islam. Among them the first was Zayd, a freed slave of the Prophet. After that Abu Bakr became a Muslim too. Abu Bakr was a well-known person. When he became a Muslim, he told every person he met about Allah. He wanted everybody to believe in Allah. Many people accepted Islam after hearing Abu Bakr speak about Allah.

Slowly the news spread. A time came when Allah said: "Muhammad ﷺ, speak loudly and openly about the Truth." The Prophet ﷺ listened to Allah's words. And he began to preach the Truth.

The Prophet Teaches in Makkah

Three years had passed since Jibril taught the Prophet ﷺ the first verses. More and more people came to know about Islam. One day Allah said to the Prophet ﷺ: "Speak of the Truth openly. This is an order."

The Prophet Muhammad ﷺ said to
Ali: "Call all the men of the Quraysh.
Call all the men who are related to my
grandfather, Abdu'l Muttalib."

Ali said to the men of the Quraysh: "Muhammad ﷺ is calling you. Come and hear what Muhammad ﷺ has to say."

42

The Prophet said to the Quraysh: "Allah is the One and True God. He gave me a message. He wants all of you to pray to Him. He wants all of you to become true believers."

The Quraysh laughed at the Prophet ﷺ. They did not want to listen to him. They did not want to abandon their false gods. They did not want to hear about Allah.

The Prophet ﷺ again said to the Quraysh: "Leave your false gods. There is no god but Allah. Listen to my message. It is a message from Allah. Don't be stubborn. Submit to Allah and pray to Him." But the Qurysh refused to listen to the Prophet ﷺ.

They complained to Abu Talib, the Prophet's uncle. They said to him: "Your nephew is talking against our religion. He does not respect us. He wants us to believe in Allah. Why don't you do something about Muhammad ﷺ? Even your son, Ali, has become his follower."

Abu Talib refused to become the Prophet's enemy. He stood by the Prophet Muhammad's side. He did not accept Islam himself. But he did not let anybody harm Muhammad ﷺ either.

Then the Quraysh went to talk to other tribes living in Makkah. They said to them: "Muhammad's relatives are protecting him. We cannot do anything to him. Let us trouble his followers. Nobody will help them."

The people of Makkah began to trouble the Prophet's followers. They laughed at their Prophet ﷺ. They pushed them in the market. They beat them when they saw them alone. They did not let them pray in peace. But Allah looked after the Prophet ﷺ and his followers. Allah gave them strength.

Some Believers go to Abyssinia

One day Allah said to the Prophet Muhammad ﷺ: "You are the Messenger of Allah. Tell people about the Truth. Tell them to believe in Allah and pray to Him."

Muhammad ﷺ was an honest and trustworthy man. The people of Makkah respected him. He said to them: "There is no god but Allah." And many of them accepted Islam.

The Quraysh leaders did not like it. They wanted the Prophet Muhammad ﷺ to stop talking to people about Allah. The Prophet Muhammad's uncle, Abu Talib, did not let the Quraysh harm him. But the other believers were not so lucky. They were poor. And they did not have powerful relatives. So the Quraysh treated them very badly.

The Prophet Muhammad ﷺ knew that Allah was looking after him. He also knew that his uncle was supporting him. But the Prophet ﷺ could not protect his followers.

He said to them: "Go to Abyssinia. The King, Negus, is a good man. He is a Christian. He believes in One God and he will look after you." The next day 83 men and 18 women including their children left Makkah.

Among them was Uthman ibn 'Affan with his wife Ruqayya, who was the daughter of the Prophet ﷺ. They went to the kingdom of Negus. The king welcomed them and let them live in his kingdom. And there they were safe.

When the Quraysh came to know about this, they became very angry. They sent two men to Abyssinia, who took gifts for the king and his generals. They said to the generals: "Tell your king to send back the Muslims."

Negus was a God-fearing man and did not listen to his generals. He told the Quraysh: "The Muslims are under my protection. I will let them live in my kingdom." Then he called the Muslims to his palace. All his ministers and bishops were there.

He told the Muslims: "Read from your scriptures. I want to hear what is written there."

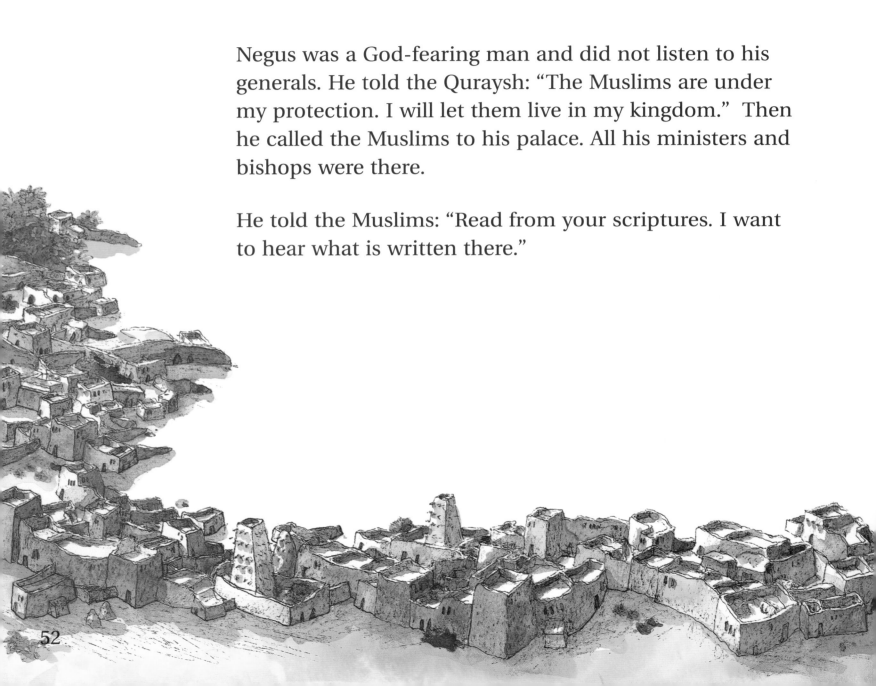

The Muslims had with them the Surah Maryam. They read it to the king and his bishops, who listened attentively. They were so touched that they cried. They said: "This is really the truth!"

Negus let the Muslims stay in Abyssinia. They lived there for many years and Allah looked after them.

'Umar accepts Islam

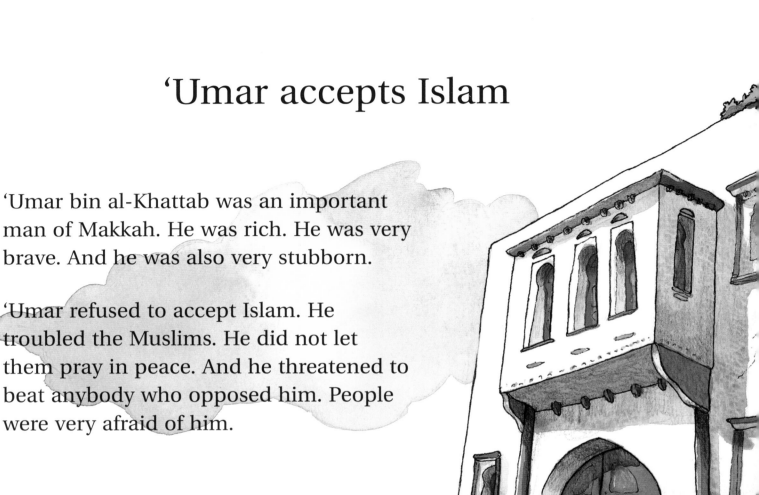

'Umar bin al-Khattab was an important man of Makkah. He was rich. He was very brave. And he was also very stubborn.

'Umar refused to accept Islam. He troubled the Muslims. He did not let them pray in peace. And he threatened to beat anybody who opposed him. People were very afraid of him.

One day the Prophet ﷺ and his followers gathered in a house to pray. 'Umar came to know about it. Sword in hand, he rushed towards the house. A man saw him walking in haste and asked him: "Where are you going with a sword in your hand?" 'Umar said: "I am going to kill Muhammad. He is spreading mischief among our people."

The man said to 'Umar: "If you kill Muhammad ﷺ, his tribe will kill you. Let him be. It would be better if you saw what is happening in your own family." "What is the matter with my family?" asked 'Umar. The man answered: "Your sister and her husband have become Muslims. And you know nothing about it!"

'Umar turned around and ran to his sister's house. He stopped outside the door and listened. He could hear somebody reading aloud. He pushed the door open and went in.

'Umar's sister hid the paper from which they were reading. Seeing this, 'Umar became so angry that he hit his sister. Then he hit his brother-in-law.

He said: "Have you become Muslims?" They were afraid of 'Umar but loved Allah best. They said: "Yes. We are Muslims. We believe in Allah and His Prophet. Do what you like."

57

When 'Umar saw that he had hurt his sister, he became ashamed. He said to her: "Give me that paper. Let me read what is written there."

He read the verses and said: "These words are truly beautiful. Lead me to Muhammad ﷺ. I want to accept Islam."

'Umar turned around and went to meet Muhammad ﷺ. He said to him: "O Messenger of Allah, I have come to tell you that I believe in Allah." The Prophet embraced him. Thus Islam was strengthen by 'Umar bin al-Khattab becoming a Muslim.

The Night Journey

One night the Prophet  was sleeping next to the Kabah. Suddenly he felt that somebody was trying to wake him up. He opened his eyes and looked up. It was the Angel Jibril. He had with him a winged horse named Buraq.

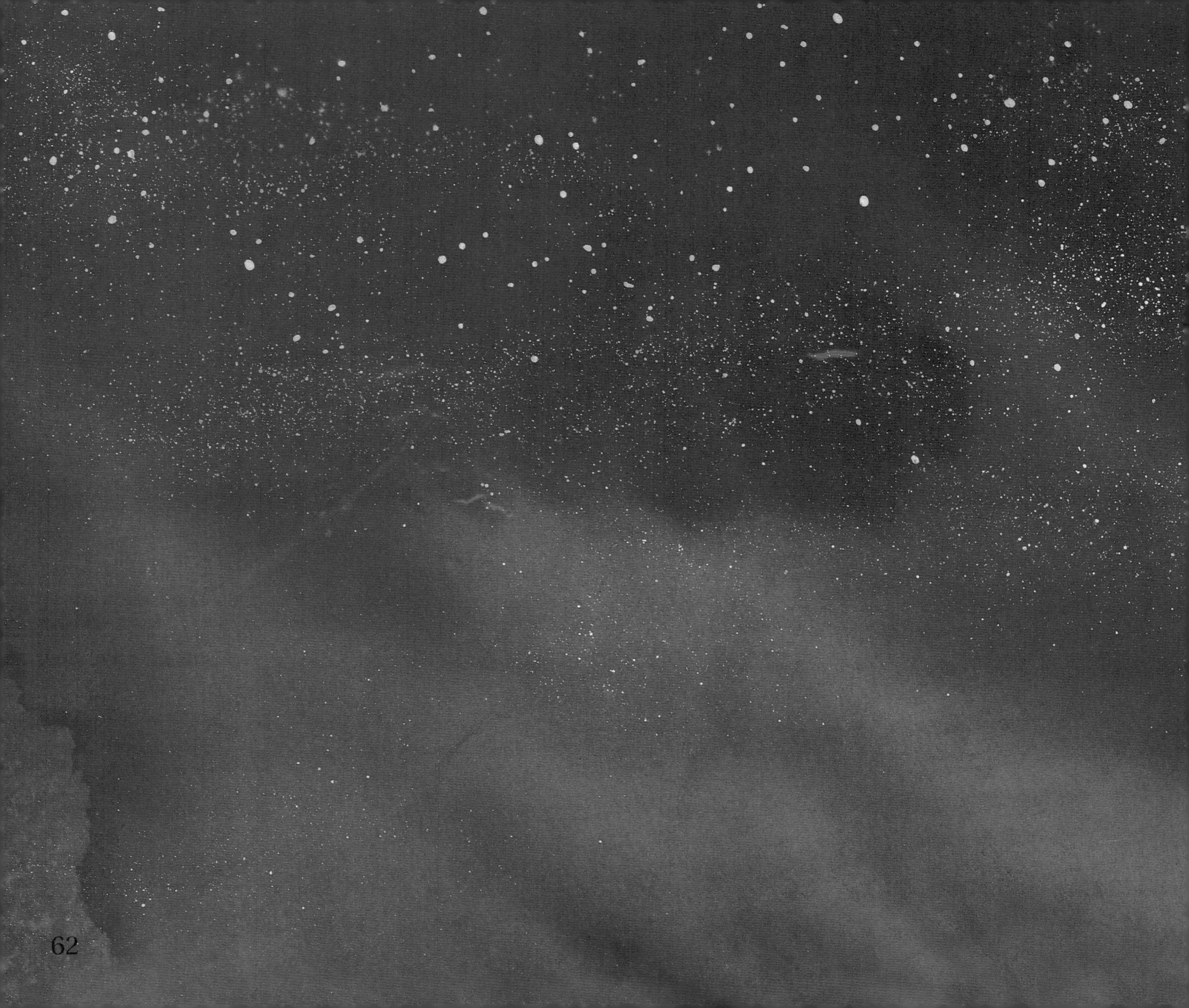

The Prophet Muhammad ﷺ mounted Buraq and then Jibril took him to Jerusalem. When they reached Jerusalem, they went to Masjid al-Aqsa. And the Prophet prayed there.

From there, they went to heaven. There were many angels walking around. All the angels smiled at the Prophet except one. The angel who did not smile was called Malik. He is the Keeper of Hell.

The Prophet Muhammad ﷺ asked Jibril: "Can you ask Malik to show me Hell?" Jibril ordered Malik to do so, and when he removed the cover from Hell, the flames blazed high into the air!

From there Jibril took the Prophet ﷺ to higher heavens. He met the earlier prophets. He met Isa, and Yahya. He met Yusuf, Idris and Musa. At the entrance to the highest heaven, he saw Abraham.

Jibril took him to Paradise. And there the Prophet ﷺ came face to face with Allah! Then the Prophet ﷺ returned to Makkah. In the morning he told the Quraysh what had happened.

Most of them said: "You are lying. It takes one month to reach Syria. And one month more to return to Makkah from there. How could you do it in one night?"

They went to Abu Bakr and asked him: "What do you think? Muhammad ﷺ is saying he went at night to Jerusalem. He even prayed there, he says!"

Abu Bakr said to them: "If Muhammad ﷺ says so, then it is true." Muhammad ﷺ was pleased with Abu Bakr. He was pleased that Abu Bakr believed in Allah and in Allah's messenger. And he called Abu Bakr "al-Siddiq", which means the Truthful One.

The Prophet and the Blind Man

One day the Prophet Muhammad ﷺ was sitting near the Kabah as usual. People gathered around him and he started explaining passages from the Qur'an to them.

Most of the people sitting with him were well dressed. They looked rich. And they looked important. Some of them were listening to the Prophet ﷺ. But most of them were arguing with him.

A man made his way towards them. He was walking slowly. He had a stick in his hand to support himself. Obviously he was poor. And he was blind.

The blind man could not see the important people. He could not see that they were well dressed. He could not see that they were the leaders of the tribe. But he could hear the Prophet's ﷺ voice. He could hear the words of the Qur'an. And he was drawn towards the voice.

He said to the Prophet ﷺ: "Messenger of Allah! Teach me all that Allah has taught you!"

The Prophet ﷺ frowned with annoyance. He said: "Don't interrupt me. I am busy." And turned his back to him. Allah did not like this. He totally disapproved of the way the Prophet ﷺ had treated the blind man. And He sent a revelation to let him know of His displeasure.

This is what Allah said to the Prophet ﷺ: "You frowned and turned your back when the blind man came. How could you tell? Maybe he was trying to purify himself. Maybe he was forewarned and could have profited from Our warning. But you were all attention to the wealthy man.

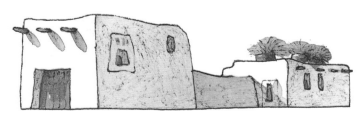

Though it would have not been your fault if the wealthy man did not purify himself. Yet you paid no heed to one who came to you with zeal and awe. Indeed, this is an admonition. And let him who will, bear it in mind." (Surah Abasa, 80:1-12)

It makes no difference to Allah if the people who love Him are rich or poor. All are equal in His eyes. Allah can see into every heart. He knows every intention. And He loves those who eagerly come to seek His guidance.

The Prophet Muhammad ﷺ and the People of Thaqif

Two people in Makkah supported the Prophet more than anyone else. One was his faithful wife, Khadijah. And the other was his uncle, Abu Talib.

The Prophet Muhammad ﷺ talked a lot to Khadijah. When he told her about all his problems and when people were mean to him, she would console him. And she always said: "Don't be unhappy. Don't despair. Allah is with you and He will help you."

Abu Talib, the Prophet's uncle, protected the Prophet ﷺ from the Quraysh. He defended him when the Quraysh spoke against him. But Khadijah and Abu Talib died soon after each other. And the Prophet ﷺ missed their support and friendship.

When Abu Talib died, the Quraysh became very rude to the Prophet ﷺ. One day when the Prophet ﷺ was walking along in the street, a young man threw dust on his head.

Nobody had dared to do anything like this as long as Abu Talib was alive.

The Prophet ﷺ went home. His head was covered in dust. When his little daughter saw him, she started to cry. But the Prophet ﷺ said: "Don't cry, little girl. Allah will protect your father."

The Prophet ﷺ could not find help in Makkah. So he went to the town of Ta'if. The tribe of the Thaqif lived there. He asked them to help him against the Quraysh. But the leaders of the Thaqif mocked him. They mocked Allah and His Prophet ﷺ!

They summoned their slaves. And they also summoned some bad and good-for-nothing men. They said to them: "We don't care for Muhammad. We don't like what he says. Why don't you beat him up and run him out of the city."

A big crowd came together. They started to insult the Prophet ﷺ. They pushed him around, and even hit him. So he had to run and hide in an orchard. Then at night he made his way back to Makkah.

When he reached safety, he prayed: "Allah! O Most Merciful! You are the Lord of the weak. You are my Lord! You are my refuge! There is no power and no might save in You."

The Pledge of Aqaba

Some distance from Makkah there was a city called Yathrib. (It is now called Madinah). The people of Yathrib heard about the Prophet ﷺ living in Makkah. They wanted to know more about Islam. One day some of them came to attend a fair in Makkah. The Prophet ﷺ was there also. They met him at a place called al-'Aqaba. The Prophet ﷺ asked them to sit down. He told them: "There is only one God. His name is Allah. He is the Lord of the Worlds. He chose me to give His message to the people. Those who listen to Allah's message will go to Paradise." And the Prophet ﷺ recited to them from the Quran. The people from Yathrib listened to the Prophet ﷺ. And they became Muslims. The Prophet called them the Helpers. When the Helpers returned home, they told other people about Islam.

In the following year there was again a fair at al-Aqaba. Twelve Helpers came for the fair. They met the Prophet ﷺ and gave him their pledge. They promised to believe in the one and only Allah. When the Helpers were going back, the Prophet ﷺ said to them: "I will send a man with you. His name is Mus'ab. He will read the Quran to you. And he will tell you about Islam." Mus'ab went to Yathrib. He lived in the house of one of the Helpers. They called him 'The Reader'. The next year the Helpers, or Ansar, came to the fair with other pilgrims of their tribe. They performed the hajj pilgrimage. At night they went to meet the Prophet ﷺ. They met him at al-Aqaba. All together they numbered 73 men and 2 women. They were from the tribes of the Khazraj

and the Aus. The Prophet ﷺ came with his uncle Al-Abbas. Al-Abbas said: "People of Khazraj. I protect Muhammad ﷺ from the Quraysh. Be sure to protect him as you would protect your own women and children." The Prophet ﷺ recited the Quran. Then he said: "Believe in Allah. And believe in the message He gave me. Accept Islam. Offer allegiance to me. And protect me as you would protect your women and children."

The men took the Prophet's hand. And they said: "By Allah who sent you with the Truth, we will protect you. We will protect you as we protect our women. We pledge our allegiance to you."

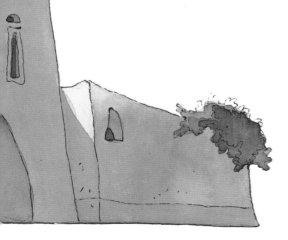

Thus the Helpers of Yathrib pledged themselves to the Prophet. This was called the second pledge of al-'Aqaba. Later on Muslims had to leave Makkah. The Helpers welcomed them to their city. Yathrib later came to be known as Madinah.

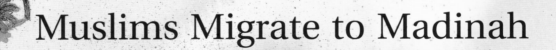

Muslims Migrate to Madinah

The Quraysh became insolent towards Allah and rejected the message Allah gave to the Prophet ﷺ. They accused the Prophet Muhammad ﷺ of lying, and mistreated him and his followers.

The life of the Muslims in Makkah became very difficult. They were insulted and even attacked. If they tried to pray in peace, they were beaten.

Allah is All-Seeing and All-Hearing. He saw the plight of the Muslims. He saw the misery of the believers. And He decided to help them. He said to the Prophet: "Allah helps those who help Him."

The Prophet ﷺ said to his followers: "Go to Madinah. Go and stay with the Ansar, that is, the Helpers. The Ansar believe in Allah. They promised to help us. They will look after you. They will become your brothers. And you can stay in their houses."

The Muslims of Makkah left for Madinah. They did not go all together and at the one time. They went in small groups. They did not want the Quraysh to know about their departure. If the Quraysh had known about it, they would not have let them go in peace.

The Ansars welcomed the Muslims. They treated them like brothers. Each family of Ansars put up one family of Muslims in their house. They shared their food with them. And they looked after them.

The Prophet ﷺ stayed back in Makkah. Allah did not give him permission to leave. Only Abu Bakr and Ali stayed back with him. All the other Muslims migrated to Madinah. When the Quraysh came to know that all the Muslims had gone to Madinah, they became very angry. They were also angry that the Ansars were helping them. Now they thought: "The Prophet ﷺ is going to go too. He will escape to Madinah. We must do something about it." And they decided to attack and kill him.

But at night the angel Jibril came to the Prophet ﷺ. He told him: "Don't sleep at night in your bed." Ali slept in the Prophet's bed and the Prophet ﷺ left the house unseen. He went straight to Abu Bakr. Both of them left Makkah and reached Madinah safely. Thus Allah looks after His own people.

The Prophet Leaves Makkah

All the Muslims left for Madinah. Only Abu Bakr and Ali were left with the Prophet ﷺ. Abu Bakr asked the Prophet again and again: "Let me go to Madinah." But the Prophet did not let him go. He said to Abu Bakr: "Don't be in a hurry. Maybe you will not have to go alone. Maybe Allah will give you a companion for your travel."

Abu Bakr thought: "Maybe Allah wants me to stay with the Prophet ﷺ. Maybe He wants me to travel when the Prophet ﷺ travels. Let me make preparations for two people." So he went and bought two camels.

He looked after them and gave them fodder every day. The camels were made ready to travel even at a moment's notice.

The Quraysh were very angry when the Muslims escaped to Madinah. They thought: "The Prophet is also going to escape. He talks all the time about Allah. He is against our customs. If other tribes support him, then we will become nothing. We must do something." And they decided to attack his house at night.

Jibril came to the Prophet ﷺ and said: "Don't sleep at night in your bed." The Prophet told Ali: "Lie down on my bed. Wrap yourself in my cloak."

At night the Quraysh surrounded the house. Nobody could leave the house. But Allah helped His Prophet ﷺ. The Prophet ﷺ came out of the house at night, and in the darkness of the night he went straight to the house of Abu Bakr. They both mounted the camels, and left the city. But they did not go straight to Madinah. Instead, they went to a nearby mountain. There was a cave there and they hid in it. In the morning Ali got up from the Prophet's bed. The Quraysh saw that they had been deceived. They shouted: "Muhammad has escaped! Let's chase him and catch him!"

The Prophet ﷺ and Abu Bakr stayed in the cave. The men who were looking for them passed by, but did not notice them. Three days later they left for Madinah, and, with Allah's help, reached there safely.

The Prophet Hides in the Cave

All the Muslims of Makkah migrated to Madinah. Only the Prophet Muhammad ﷺ and Abu Bakr were left. The Prophet was waiting for Allah to give him permission to leave. Finally, one day Jibril came to him and said: "Do not sleep in your bed tonight."

The night fell. Ali and the Prophet Muhammad ﷺ were alone in the house. Suddenly they heard some noise outside. They looked out, and saw the enemies of the Prophet surrounding the house. The Prophet ﷺ was not afraid. He knew Allah was with him. He told Ali: 'Lie down in my bed and cover yourself with my cloak. I am going to leave with Abu Bakr. You follow later on."

The Prophet ﷺ quickly left his house at night. In the pitch darkness he went to Abu Bakr's house where Abu Bakr had two camels ready. They mounted the camels and left the city. They made for Mount Thawr, which was nearby. There was a cave there, in which they hid.

92

They stayed in the cave for three days. Every night Abu Bakr's son, Abdullah, came to meet them. He brought the news of what was happening in the city. Abdullah told them: "The Quraysh of Makkah are very angry. They are looking for you everywhere. They are even offering a reward of a hundred camels to the man who captures you."

One day they heard some voices outside the cave. It was a search party of the Quraysh who were looking for them. Abu Bakr was stricken with fear. He thought: "We will be discovered any time now." But the Prophet ﷺ said: "Do not despair, Allah is with us." The men looked around and moved away. Nobody had bothered to look into the cave!

After staying for three days in the cave, when it was safe, they left the cave. They hired a guide to take them across the desert to Madinah. It took seven days to reach Madinah.

Suraqa Bin Malik Chases the Prophet

The Quraysh were enraged when the Prophet Muhammad ﷺ migrated to Madinah. They offered a reward for his capture. They said: "We will give a hundred camels to anyone who brings him back."

Many men were tempted by the reward. They jumped on their camels and horses and rode into the desert. They looked for the Prophet ﷺ and his companion. But they could find no trace of them anywhere.

One day Suraqa bin Malik was sitting with some men of his

tribe. A man stopped by and said: "I have seen three riders. It must have been Muhammad and Abu Bakr with their guide."

Suraqa bin Malik made a sign to him to keep quiet and said: "These men are looking for a lost camel. I know them. They are certainly not Muhammad and Abu Bakr."

After a while Suraqa got up and went home. He took his weapons and mounted his horse. He thought: "Let me catch Muhammad and Abu Bakr. I could do with a reward. And a hundred camels is a handsome reward indeed."

Suraqa rode into the desert. He was a great rider and he soon caught up with Muhammad ﷺ and Abu Bakr. But as he came near, his horse stumbled and threw him down. He got up and remounted. After a few paces the horse stumbled again. Again he found himself on the ground! Undeterred, he got hold of the horse and jumped on to it. The horse stumbled for the third time. And threw him off yet again!

Suraqa thought: "God is protecting Muhammad. Nothing is going to harm him." And he called out to the Prophet: "This is Suraqa bin Malik! Wait for me! I won't harm you!"

Abu Bakr asked: "What do you want?" Suraqa said: "Write a document. Let it be a sign between the Prophet and me." Abu Bakr wrote out a document and gave it to him.

Suraqa Bin Malik meets the Prophet again

Many years had passed since the migration to Madinah and the Prophet Muhammad ﷺ was now returning to Makkah. People crowded to see the Prophet ﷺ. And the Ansar had to stop them from mobbing the Prophet ﷺ.

Suraqa bin Malik was in the crowd. He wanted to see the Prophet ﷺ again. He remembered how he had chased the Prophet ﷺ across the desert.

This had happened when the Prophet ﷺ and Abu Bakr were migrating from Makkah. The Quraysh offered a reward for bringing the Prophet ﷺ back. Suraqa was keen to get the reward which was a hundred camels. So he chased the Prophet ﷺ and caught up with him in the desert.

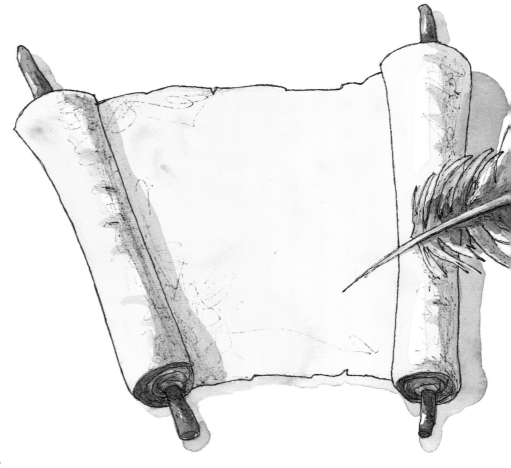

But when he was near the Prophet ﷺ, his horse stumbled. Suraqa found himself on the ground. He got back on to the horse and yelled to the horse to run fast. But the horse stumbled again. This happened three times. By then Suraqa knew: "Allah is protecting the Prophet. Nothing can harm him." He cried to the Prophet ﷺ and Abu Bakr: "I will not harm you. Just write a letter for me. I want a sign of having met the Prophet."

Now, many years later, the Ansar would not let him near the Prophet ﷺ.

He shouted: "This is Suraqa bin Malik!" And he held up his letter signed by the Prophet ﷺ above his head. All could see it. The Prophet ﷺ saw him too.

He called out: "Let him through. Today is the day of repayment and goodness." Suraqa approached the Prophet ﷺ. He was overwhelmed and accepted Islam there and then.

Then Suraqa remembered something he wanted to ask the Prophet ﷺ. He said: "Stray camels used to come to my water tank. I kept it full of water for my camels. But I let the stray camels drink there too. Shall I get a reward for having let them have water?"

"Yes," replied the Prophet ﷺ. "There is a reward for watering every thirsty creature."

The Prophet comes to Madinah

It was a difficult time for the Muslims of Makkah. Their enemies troubled them all the time. They did not let them pray in peace. They abused them. Sometimes they even attacked them. So the Prophet Muhammad ﷺ told them to go to Madinah (which was known as Yathrib at that time).

Madinah was a city some distance from Makkah. Its inhabitants had heard of the Prophet Muhammad ﷺ, so they came to Makkah to meet him. On meeting him, they became Muslims. And they invited the Prophet ﷺ and his followers to come to Madinah. They wanted them to live with them.

First the Prophet ﷺ sent his followers. He did not go himself, but waited for a sign from Allah. One day Jibril came and told him: "Don't go to sleep tonight."

The Prophet's ﷺ enemies surrounded his house that night. The Prophet ﷺ saw them and told Ali: "Sleep on my bed. And cover yourself with my cloak." Ali lay down on the Prophet's bed while the Prophet ﷺ quietly left the house.

The Prophet ﷺ went straight to Abu Bakr's house, where Abu Bakr had two camels ready for the flight. They mounted the camels and left the city. They went to a nearby mountain and hid in a cave there.

They stayed in the cave for three days. Their enemies looked for them everywhere, but could not find them. One day, some people who were looking for them, passed by the cave. They looked at the entrance to the cave, but did not go in. When they left, the Prophet ﷺ and Abu Bakr looked out. They saw a huge spider's web blocking the entrance. That is why the search party had walked by and had not bothered to go in!

Three days later the Prophet ﷺ and Abu Bakr left with a guide, who took them across the desert. He took them by a route, which only a few people knew. And he led them safely to Madinah.

Every day the people of Madinah stood outside the city. They looked towards the desert and waited for the Prophet ﷺ. They waited for many days, but he did not come. He came finally on a hot afternoon. He stopped in the shade of a palm tree and the people greeted him. They were happy he was among them at last.

The first sermon which the Prophet ﷺ gave to the people of Madinah has been recorded in the books of Hadith, as "*Awwalu Khutbatin Khatabaha Rasulullahi Sallallahu alayhi wa sallam fil Madinah*".
In this sermon the Prophet ﷺ did not say a word against the people of Makkah who had prosecuted him and driven him out of the city.
The Prophet ﷺ simply warned the people of Madinah about Hellfire and reminded them of the Day of Judgement, when every soul would stand in front of the Almighty to be judged and rewarded or punished according his or her deeds.

The Constitution of Madinah

The Prophet ﷺ and his followers settled in Madinah. The Muslims who came with the Prophet were called the Muhajirun. It means the Emigrants. They were called the Emigrants because they migrated from Makkah. The Muslims who were the natives of Madinah were called the Ansar. The Ansar means the Helpers.

The Emigrants came to Madinah from Makkah. They had no houses in Madinah. And they brought only the most necessary things with them. But the Helpers were natives of Madinah. They had houses there. They had fields and orchards.

The Prophet ﷺ told the Muslims: "The Emigrants and the Helpers are brothers. All the Muslims belong to one family. They must help each other. They must look after each other." And the Helpers put up the Emigrants in their own houses. They gave them food. They shared with them whatever they had.

In Madinah there also lived a large number of Jews. The Prophet ﷺ said: "The Jews are the People of the Book." And he made a friendly agreement with them.

The agreement was written down. This is what it said:
"In the name of Allah, the Compassionate, the Merciful.
This is an agreement with Muhammad, the Prophet. It is
an agreement between all communities of Madinah. It is
an agreement between both Muslims and non-Muslims."

"The Jews have their religion and the Muslims have theirs. The Muslims will respect the rights of the Jews. They will protect them. And the Jews will be loyal to the Muslims and fight by their side. In this way, all those who stay in Madinah will be one community."

"Madinah shall be a sanctuary for the people of this document. If there is any misunderstanding, the final judges shall be the Prophet ﷺ and Allah. But this document will protect only just and honest people. It will not protect unjust people and sinners."

"Allah is the protector of the good. Allah is the protector of the God-fearing. And Muhammad ﷺ is the Messenger of Allah."

Muhammad ﷺ, the Prophet of Allah, was the leader of Madinah. All the people of Madinah were guaranteed their rights. And they knew their duties. Both Muslims and non-Muslims were told how to live together.

They were told how to live in peace.

The Call to Prayer

The Muslims settled in Madinah. They followed Islam in whatever they did. They prayed. They fasted. And they gave alms.

The Prophet led the prayers. People gathered around him without being called. When the time for prayers came, they just came and prayed with the Prophet.

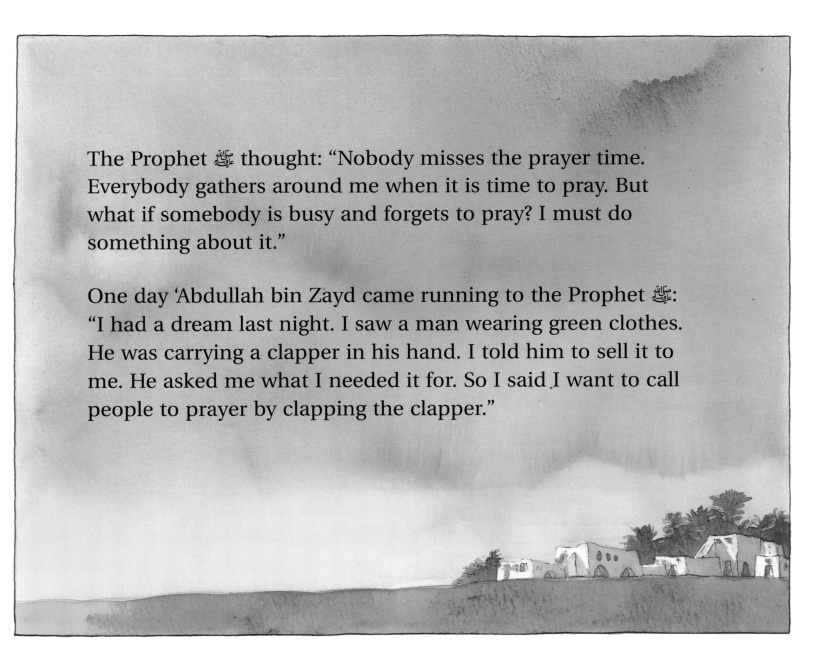

The Prophet ﷺ thought: "Nobody misses the prayer time. Everybody gathers around me when it is time to pray. But what if somebody is busy and forgets to pray? I must do something about it."

One day 'Abdullah bin Zayd came running to the Prophet ﷺ: "I had a dream last night. I saw a man wearing green clothes. He was carrying a clapper in his hand. I told him to sell it to me. He asked me what I needed it for. So I said I want to call people to prayer by clapping the clapper."

"The man said to me: 'I will show you a better way. Just simply call out twice:

Allah is Most Great, Allah is Most Great.

I bear witness that there is no deity other than Allah.

I bear witness that Muhammad ﷺ is the Messenger of Allah.

Come to prayer.

Come to success.

Allah is Most Great, Allah is Most Great (once).

There is no deity other than Allah (once).'"

The Prophet ﷺ listened to 'Abdullah bin Zayd. Then he said: "It is a true dream from Allah. Go and look for Bilal. His voice is loud and clear. Tell him to call people to prayer with the words you heard in the dream."

The mosque of the Prophet ﷺ had no minaret. So Bilal climbed on to the roof of the highest house nearby. And he gave the call to prayer.

'Umar was in his house when he heard the *adhan*. He hurried to the house of the Prophet ﷺ and said: "I had the same dream last night." And the Prophet ﷺ answered: "Allah be praised!"

Bilal was the first muezzin. Every muezzin since then calls people to prayer in the same words. Five times a day people hear the *adhan* and come to pray. They pray wherever they are. They pray in every corner of the world.

The Change of Qibla

Almost eighteen months had passed since the Prophet ﷺ came to Madinah. He stayed in the house of Abu Ayyub, a Helper. Immediately, he ordered his followers to build a mosque. Both the Helpers and the Emigrants worked hard. Soon the mosque was ready. And near the mosque stood the Prophet's house.

The mosque of the Prophet ﷺ was very simple. The enclosure was made of palm tree trunks. And the roof of palm tree leaves.

The Prophet ﷺ led all the prayers in the mosque. At first, Jerusalem was the *qibla,* or the prayer direction. The Prophet ﷺ and his followers prayed facing Jerusalem. Then one day a revelation came to the Prophet ﷺ while he was praying. Allah ordered him to change the *qibla.*

This is how it happened: The Prophet ﷺ was leading the prayers. He was facing Jerusalem as usual. While in the middle of the prayer, he suddenly received a revelation of the Quran.

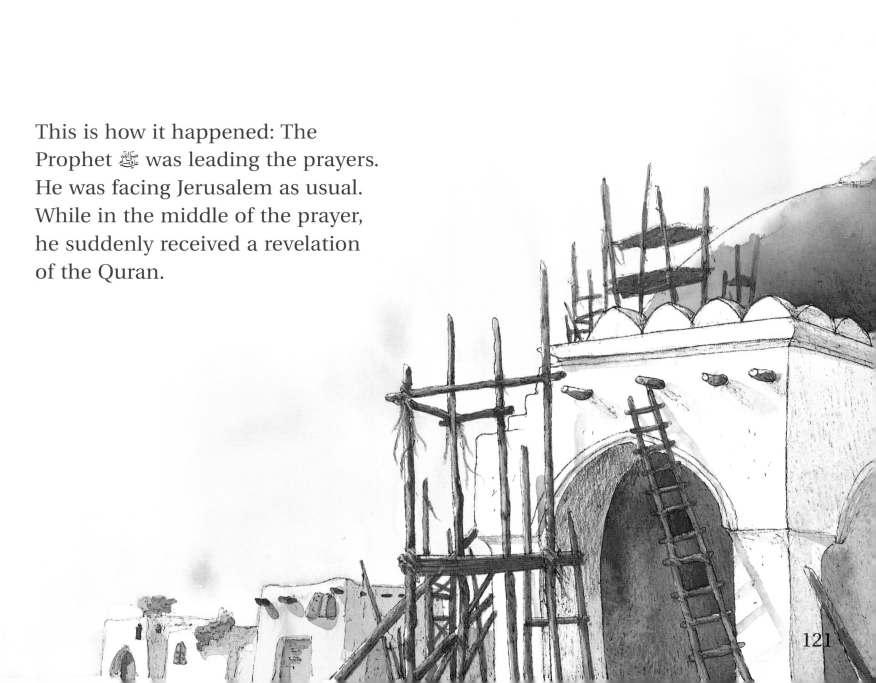

The following were the words of the revelation: "I have often seen you look at the sky. I have seen you search the heavens. Now I will give you a *qibla* that will make you happy. Turn your face towards the Sacred Mosque. And pray facing the Kabah."

The Prophet ﷺ turned there and then. The people followed him. They began the prayers facing Jerusalem. But they finished the prayers facing the Kabah. To this day, a mosque in Madinah stands at the very spot where this revelation was made. It is called, Masjid al-Qiblatayn or "The Mosque of Two Qiblas".

The Women of Ansar

The Qur'an was revealed to the Prophet Muhammad ﷺ. But it was not all revealed at the one time. The first revelation happened in the cave of Hira. The Prophet ﷺ was sitting alone. Suddenly the Angel Jibril appeared before him. He said to the Prophet ﷺ: "Recite!" And taught him the very first verses from the Quran.

The revelations continued till the Prophet's death. Some revelations took place when the Prophet ﷺ lived in Makkah. And some took place after he had to migrate to Madinah. The Muslims of Madinah were called the Ansar or the Helpers.

They accepted Islam and asked the Prophet ﷺ to come and live with them. The Muslims who came from Makkah were called the Muhajirun, or the Emigrants.

The Helpers and the Emigrants lived together in Madinah. They were like brothers. The Ansar men obeyed every command of the Prophet ﷺ. They tried to please Allah in everything. And the Ansar women were as obedient and as pious.

One day it happened that the following verse, addressed to the women, was revealed: "They should draw their veils over their bosoms." (Surah al-Noor, 31) The men of the Ansar heard the verse. They immediately returned to their homes. They told their mothers, wives and sisters: "Allah sent a command for you. Cover yourselves with veils."

The women of the Ansar stopped whatever they were doing. They got up. One untied her waist-belt. Another took a sheet. They made veils out of them and put them on.

The next day in the morning, when they said their prayers behind the Prophet ﷺ, all of them had scarves on their heads. Indeed, said Aisha, the wife of the Prophet ﷺ, there were no women better than the women of the Ansar. They honoured the Book of Allah. And they had full faith in all it said.

The Daughters of the Prophet ﷺ

The Prophet Muhammad ﷺ had four daughters. All of them were born in Makkah. Their mother was Khadija. The eldest daughter, Zaynab, was married to her cousin, Abu'l As. Ruqayya and Umm Kulthum were married to Uthman bin Affan (the third caliph of Islam); he married Ruqayya first, and after she died, he married her sister Umm Kulthum. Fatimah was the youngest. When she grew up she was married to Ali. Ali was the first young person to convert to Islam.

Ali, the son of Abu Talib, related how Fatimah, his wife and also daughter of the Prophet Muhammad ﷺ, had to do all the housework herself. Her hands used to become blistered from working a millstone, her clothes became dirty from sweeping the floor, and she had a mark on her neck from having to bring water from far away in a large leather bag.

Once when the Prophet ﷺ had many servants come to him, 'Ali suggested to Fatimah that she go and request her father to give her one of them. But there were many people gathered at his house, so she returned home without meeting him. The next day the Prophet ﷺ came to the house of 'Ali and Fatimah and asked what she had wanted to discuss, but Fatimah remained silent.

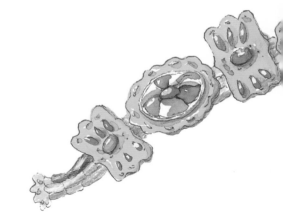

Then 'Ali told the Prophet  the whole story. The Prophet did not, however, say yes to their request. "Fear God," he said, "and fulfil your duty to the Lord. Continue to do your housework and, when you go

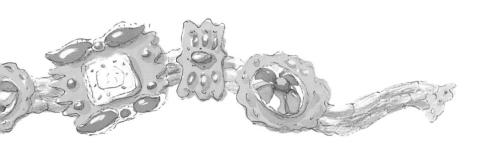

to bed at night, glorify Allah 33 times, praise Him the same number of times and exalt him 34 times. That makes 100 times altogether. That will do you more good than a servant will."

Books for Little Hearts!

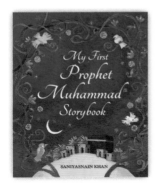

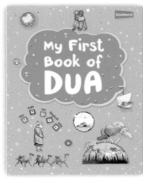

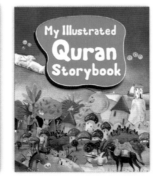

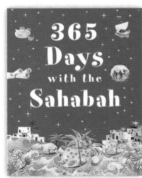

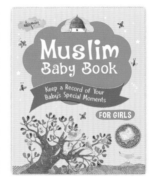

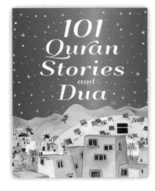

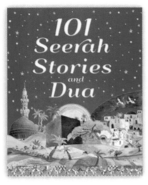

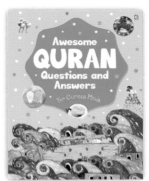